How to Play Guzheng, the Chinese Zither
– the Basic Skills

H.H. Lee

A guide to playing guzheng, the Chinese zither at home by yourself

How to Play Guzheng, the Chinese Zither - the Basic Skills, Edition 1.1

ISBN: 9781973409199

Table of Contents

Preface

Guzheng (古箏), or simply Zheng (箏), is a Chinese plucked string instrument with a history of more than 2 500 years. Guzheng literally means "ancient zheng", in which the word "zheng" either is onomatopoeia or derives from a tale of two brothers who fought for it[1]. Legend has it that guzheng was used as a weapon in the Warring States Period of ancient China, but later developed into a musical instrument after strings were attached to it. Known as the Chinese zither in the West, guzheng belongs to the plucking family[2] in the modern Chinese orchestra[3].

Guzheng/古箏

Guzheng might have a common origin with zhu (筑), another plucked string instrument in one of the seven warrior states, the State of Chu (楚

---

[1] The Chinese terms for the words "fighting for" (爭) and "zheng" (箏) are homophones.

[2] The plucking family mainly consists of pipa (琵琶), liuqin (柳琴), ruans (soprano, alto, tenor and bass) (阮), sanxian (三弦), guzheng (古箏) and yangqin (揚琴).

[3] The modern Chinese orchestra consists of four families, namely the bowing (bowed string), the plucking (plucked string), the blowing (wind) and the hitting (percussion).

國), because their bodies shared the same design and just differed in the number of strings (guzheng had five strings while zhu had 13 strings). There was also another instrument called Se (瑟) at that time, similar to them but with 25 strings and larger in size. As time passed, wood replaced bamboo as the material for making the guzheng, whereas the number of strings increased to 13 in the Tang Dynasty and further to 21 in the modern times.

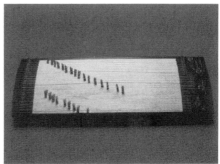

Zhu/筑 (left) and Se/瑟 (right)

The elegance of sound, wide range of notes and variety of playing skills all help to render the guzheng as a favorite of the Chinese people and an emblematic element of the Chinese culture.

In the following, I will show you how to play the guzheng. Even if you are an amateur of Chinese music, you can still play some simple songs with enough efforts. Remember, practice makes perfect! But the first thing to do, doubtlessly, is to choose a guzheng.

The Structure of the Guzheng

I will illustrate the guzheng structure with a 21-stringed guzheng as shown below:

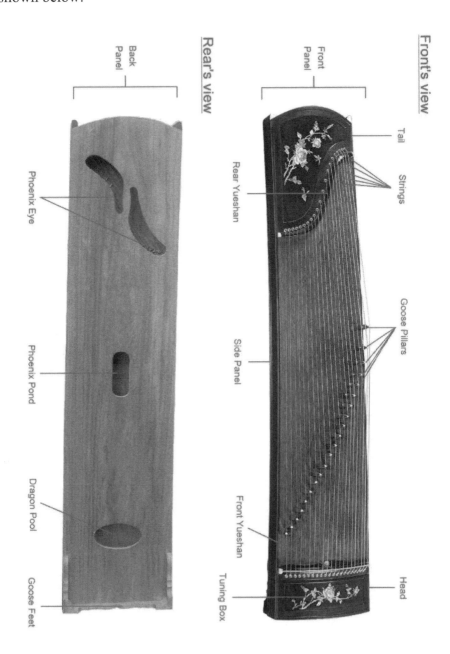

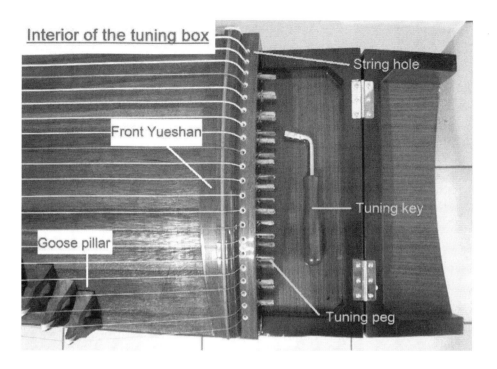

Interior of the tuning box

The dimensions of a 21-stringed guzheng are normally 163 cm in length, 35 cm (head)/ 30 cm (tail) in width, and 8 cm in thickness. Most parts of a guzheng are made of wood, with their functions shown as follows:

Name	Description
Front panel	The front panel forms the main part of the resonance body, to which most of the smaller parts are affixed.
Head	Carved with some patterns for the purpose of decoration, the head holds the tuning box and connects to the front Yueshan.
Tuning box	The tuning box contains delicate components inside with a cover for protection.
String hole	The string holes are beneath the right side of the front Yuenshan and the left side of the rear Yueshan, through which the strings pass.

Tuning peg	The tuning pegs are adjacently arranged inside the tuning box for varying the tension on the strings to adjust their pitches (the higher the tension, the higher the pitch).
Tuning key	The tuning key is used to twist the tuning pegs.
Front Yueshan	The front Yueshan is a piece of wood that hangs the strings over the front panel. A buffer is installed thereon to alleviate the pressure exerted by the strings.
String	The 21 strings of a guzheng are made of stainless steel wrapped with nylon, though other materials like silk, rayon or pure steel can also be used. They are usually tuned from D5 (the 1st string, at the bottom) to D1 (the 21st string, at the top) on the Chinese pentatonic scale in the repeated order of D, B, A, F♯ and E.
Goose pillar (nut)	The goose pillars serve as the medium for transmitting the vibrations of the strings to the front panel, and as a tool for adjusting the pitch of an individual string as well.
Rear Yueshan	The rear Yueshan, also with a buffer to divert the pressure from the strings, plays a similar role to its counterpart, the front Yueshan.
Tail	Like the head, the tail is carved with some patterns for the purpose of decoration.
Side panel	The side panels help to form the resonance body.
Back panel	The back panel resonates with the front panel and vibrates the air inside the resonance body.
Dragon pool	Also called the front sound emitting hole, the dragon pool is one of the three holes through

	which sounds are emitted. It provides a fulcrum for hanging the guzheng on the wall.
Phoenix pond	Also called the middle sound emitting hole, the phoenix pond is one of the three holes through which sounds are emitted.
Phoenix eye	Also called the rear sound emitting hole, the phoenix eye is one of the three holes through which sounds are emitted. The strings have to pass through it during replacement.
Goose feet	The goose feet elevate the guzheng above the surface on which it lies such that sounds can be clearly emitted from the aforesaid three holes.

After understanding the guzheng structure, we now have enough knowledge to choose a guzheng for ourselves.

How to Choose a Guzheng

The quality of a guzheng is influenced by three factors, viz. material, craftsmanship and timbre. For the sake of clarity, we shall look into each part of the guzheng in detail:

On the material front

The front panel

Front panels are mostly made of Chinese parasol trees (known as *Wutong* in Chinese), which are white or pale-yellow in color and soft in texture. As such, special care should be provided since unsightly scratches can be easily left thereon. The front panel can be made of a single piece or multiple pieces of wood assembled together to cater for the balance between notes of high and low pitches.

Wutong (梧桐) is an excellent material for making the front panel thanks to its superior sonic properties

As a general rule, the front panel should be ideally free of knots and cracks, and would be deemed fine if the wood grain is conspicuous with considerable width. For assembled panels, we have to scrutinize the junctions between individual pieces to ensure that there are no noticeable gaps. If the front panel has been varnished by the manufacturer, it will be quite hard to perform the inspection, however.

The side panels

The four side panels (two longer and two shorter) join the front and back panels. Among them, the longer pair of panels is crucial to the balance of the guzheng body and stability of the sound. In this connection, we should choose those made of hard wood, such as red wood and Catalpa wood, because their dense texture can withstand pressure and resist changes in temperature and humidity.

Side panels are often made of red wood in view of its dense texture

The back panel

The back panel also affects the timbre and loudness of the guzheng to a certain degree, so it is better to choose those made of good materials like Chinese parasol trees, followed by white pine and assorted pieces of wood. To identify the kind of wood used, we can examine the periphery of the sound emitting holes, since they are usually not covered by paint.

The emitting holes can be protected against fracture with a wooden frame installed upon production (left), though it is difficult to identify the kind of wood used when compared with those unprotected (right)

The Yueshans

The front (straight) and rear (curved like a letter "s" like the one shown in the left picture) Yueshans are projections that hang the strings above the front panel and help to produce crisp sounds. They are installed with a buffer to alleviate the pressure exerted by the strings.

For strings made of steel wrapped with nylon, the buffer should be ideally made of bone; for strings made of pure steel, the buffer should be made of copper wire then. Nevertheless, bamboo is used for most Yueshans now owing to its cheaper cost.

The goose pillars

At present, most of the goose pillars are made of red wood. To assess their quality, we can measure their weight as goose pillars that are abnormally lighter often turn out to be inferior. Besides, we also need to check whether the goose pillars are in close contact with the surface of the front panel, where their heights diminish evenly from high to low pitches. Their head (inverted triangle) are inlaid with other materials like hard plastic, but preferably with cow bone.

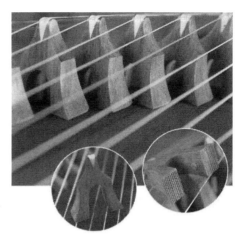

The top of the goose pillars is made of cow bone for better sound transmission, whereas anti-sliding grooves are carved at the bottom so that the pillars can grip the front panel firmly

The strings

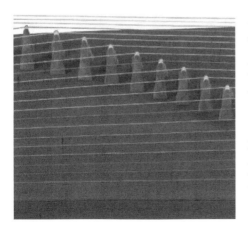

The strings should be evenly distributed on the front panel. When checking their quality, we have to pluck them each by each to listen to the sound produced. In case the majority of them produce dull sounds and resonate poorly in the low-pitched region, we have to look for another guzheng instead.

On the timbre front

Despite the same material and craftsmanship, the timbre will still fluctuate. Therefore, we should at least draw comparison between two guzhengs to see whether 1) the sounds produced by every string are mellow without noises; 2) the notes in the low, middle and high-pitched regions are balanced in volume and timbre; and 3) we feel comfortable to pluck the strings under the D major setting.

In addition, we should pay heed to two aspects: if the sounds are not loud enough even with strenuous plucking efforts by our right hand, or the strings are out of tune when they are subject to high pressure from both of our hands, the guzheng in question will be considered disqualified. Of course, it is always advisable to have someone who is familiar with guzhengs to accompany you in the course of selection.

On the craftsmanship front

The craftsmanship significantly affects the timbre, appearance and life of a guzheng, which can be identified from several subtleties like the accessories, electroplated parts, and amount of adhesive applied on the guzheng, etc.

The appearance

Decorative patterns appeal to our eye but are not necessary. Worse still, wood and jade carvings protruding from the head of a guzheng will hinder our performance. Therefore, we can choose a guzheng as long as it does not have any scratches or blemishes, with all parts properly glued and put in place, which already serves us well.

The head of the above guzheng is lavishly carved with patterns of a dragon and clouds

The adhesive

The panels of a guzheng are merely glued with adhesive, which will easily separate if the guzheng is pressurized or dampened (especially the amount of adhesive is insufficient). We can examine the joints of the panels at the sound emitting holes to check whether adequate adhesive has been applied.

The compatibility of the goose pillars with the front panel

The incongruity between the goose pillars and the front panel will influence the timbre, as sounds of striking the front panel will be heard intermittently therefrom, and eventually the front panel will be damaged. Thus, we should check the goose pillars to see whether they have been polished by the manufacturer before the guzheng is put for sale, because polished ones can grip the front panel more firmly.

The rings on the string holes

The rings should have a shiny electroplated layer to prevent rusting, and their diameter should also be large enough for the thicker strings in the low-pitched region to pass through in case of replacement. If the rings are not tightly fixed, we have to screw them deeper into the Yueshans to avoid accidental detachment.

Electroplated rings on the front Yueshan

The distance between the strings

The strings should be equally spaced out on the front panel

As mentioned before, the strings should be evenly arranged on the Yueshans, otherwise hindrance to performance will likely occur. The even arrangement of the strings hinges upon the distances between the string holes on the front Yueshan, through which the strings pass. As a result, we need to check them as well.

After choosing a suitable guzheng, it is time to learn how to play it!

How to Play the Guzheng

Good performances rely on correct playing postures. When playing the guzheng, we have to bear in mind:

<u>The posture</u>

The prevailing posture is sitting on a chair, although other postures like standing and kneeling on the ground are also possible when necessary. Normally, the guzheng is placed on two stands in the shape of a stool, but sometimes can be directly placed on the player's thighs.

When adopting the sitting posture, the guzheng is placed on the stands, with the higher one adhering to the goose feet and the shorter one overlapping the phoenix eye. The higher stand is usually 55 cm in height and 36 cm in width, while the shorter stand 50 cm in height and 33 cm in width. Adjust the position of the guzheng stably on the stands lest it would slide or even fall on the ground abruptly.

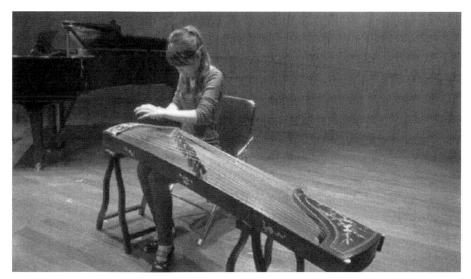

The above picture depicts a female guzheng player adopting the sitting posture

After setting the stands, we should sit on a chair with an appropriate height (around 45 to 48 cm), by which we can move our legs comfortably beneath the guzheng, and our wrists can naturally linger over the strings. At this time, our waist should also be slightly above the front panel, where our body will not incline forward (if the chair is too high), nor our arms and shoulders stretch too much (if the chair is too low).

The above picture shows a pair of guzheng stands with the higher one (left) placed under the goose feet and the shorter one (right) under the phoenix eye

The chair should face the front Yueshan at a distance of around 6 to 10 cm, as it is difficult to pluck the strings with our right hand if we sit too far away (more than 10 cm), and hard to press the strings with our left hand if we sit too close (less than 6 cm). Thereafter, we should sit still with our back straight and occupy only half of the chair. In the meantime, our left foot should be a bit in front of our right foot beneath the guzheng.

At last, relax and raise both of our arms naturally, then grip our hands and flex all fingers slightly. Lower our head a bit to look at the strings and behave decently.

Afterwards, we have to tune the guzheng so that every string of its produces the correct note. The following diagram illustrates the default arrangement of notes (with respect to their strings) on the staff:

Tuning the strings

Arrangement of Notes under the Default Setting (the D Major)

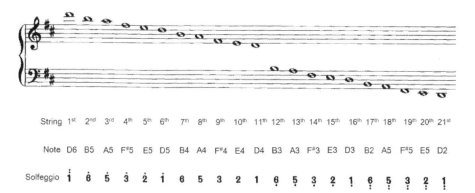

String	1st	2nd	3rd	4th	5th	6th	7th	8th	9th	10th	11th	12th	13th	14th	15th	16th	17th	18th	19th	20th	21st
Note	D6	B5	A5	F#5	E5	D5	B4	A4	F#4	E4	D4	B3	A3	F#3	E3	D3	B2	A5	F#5	E5	D2
Solfeggio	i̤	6̇	5̇	3̇	2̇	i̇	6	5	3	2	1	6̣	5̣	3̣	2̣	1̣	6̤	5̤	3̤	2̤	1̤

To tune the guzheng, first open the tuning box and connect the clip-on sensor of the tuner to a string in the way as shown in the right picture.   Pluck the string and listen to the sound produced. If the sound is out of tune, twist the corresponding tuning peg with the tuning key until the right pitch is reached (which can be determined by making reference to the above arrangement of notes on the staff).   Meanwhile, press the string with the left hand beyond its goose pillar (nut) to stabilize the pitch, whereby we can also feel the tension on the string to avoid breakage due to overstretching.   We usually start with the 7th to 11th strings that lie in the middle-pitched region, and repeat the said process for other strings in the high, low and bass-pitched regions.   Finally, close the tuning box when all the strings have been correctly tuned.

The left hand

We can either pluck or press the strings with our left hand, yet traditionally we only press the strings to embellish, beautify and alter the sounds produced by the plucking motions of the right hand.

To press the strings, first stick the index and middle fingers (or the ring finger as well) together and bend them slightly. Next, touch the strings with the fingertips to the left of the goose pillars (without changing the vibrating lengths of the strings) to cope with the plucking motions of the right hand. We need to pay attention to the following:

1)　We exert force mainly with the middle finger;

2)　We press the strings to the left of the goose pillars at a distance of 16 to 19 cm, which will be longer in the high-pitched region and shorter in the low-pitched region;

3)　The angle between the fingers and the back of the hand is around 110° when the fingers bend naturally;

4)　The left hand inclines to the front left side when we pluck the strings outward, and to our body when we pluck the strings inward;

5)　The force is transmitted from the shoulder to the hand through the arm, rather than solely from the fingers, hand or wrist;

6)   The fingers and shoulder should be on the same axis, whereas the hand and arm form a curved bow; and

7)   The thumb and little finger are separated from the index finger and ring finger respectively without tilting or drooping.

<u>The right hand</u>

We pluck the strings with our right hand, either by using one finger or multiple fingers.   There are totally eight basic techniques of plucking the strings with one finger, namely 托/*tuo*, 劈/*pi*, 抹/*mo*, 挑/*tiao*, 勾 /*gou*, 剔/*ti*, 打/*da* and 摘/*zhai* (transliteration is used for the Chinese terms due to the lack of equivalents), and by combining any two of the above techniques, we can pluck the strings with multiple fingers.

By tradition, we used to place the ring finger gently around the front Yueshan (on the 4th or 5th string away from the thumb), where it serves as a pivot on which the other fingers can easily pluck the strings. Remember that the ring finger cannot exert too much pressure on the string or overstretch, otherwise it will be difficult for the thumb to pluck the strings.

The right hand will look like an overturned flower or a chicken foot like the one shown in the above picture when we have anchored the ring finger to the string

Under normal circumstances, the thumb is 5 strings away from the middle finger, with the center of the palm hovering around the 2nd and 3rd strings counted from the thumb. Our right hand should also lean toward the right a bit instead of being perpendicular to the strings.

The fingers under the 5-string separation

With the ring finger acting as the pivot, we can exert larger force from the other fingers, in particular the thumb, to pluck the strings consecutively and rapidly. However, this is not necessary for all songs nowadays, and hence the ring finger can also take part in plucking the strings (on the other hand, the little finger is still rarely used). Among the five fingers, the thumb is the principal finger with which we pluck the strings the most.

Let's look into the plucking motions of each finger in detail:

When plucking with the thumb, we utilize the metacarpo- phalangeal joint such that the thumb will pluck the string at an angle of 45°, while our arm moves accordingly to produce solid and elegant sounds. Upon completion, the thumb will fall on the adjacent string.

For the index finger, we utilize the 1st and 2nd phalangeal joints (the mainstay) to pluck the strings downward, whereby harmonizing with the sounds produced with the thumb and middle finger. Don't twist the wrist in order to pluck violently.

Same as the thumb, we utilize the metacarpophalangeal joint of the middle finger to pluck the strings inward at an angle of 45°, which somewhat inclines to the direction of the front Yueshan. Upon completion, the middle finger will leave at the adjacent string.

As mentioned before, the ring finger sometimes acts as a pivot. When we are going to pluck the string to which it is anchored with other fingers, we should raise it to avoid touching the string. Having said that, we can still pluck the strings with it by utilizing the phalangeal joints like the index finger on few occasions. Meanwhile, the little finger virtually does not engage in any plucking motions, so we often need to raise it a bit to avoid touching any strings accidentally.

Plucking the strings from the low-pitched to high-pitched region can be visualized as if we were drawing a diagonal line to the left of the front Yueshan, since the distances between the position where we pluck the strings and the front Yueshan for the low-pitched and high-pitched regions are usually 7.5 and 3.5 cm respectively, although these distances may vary to meet the specific requirements of different songs.

A set of four false nails (excluding the little finger) can be obtained at a very low price from the Internet

Last but not least, we should also wear false nails to prevent our own ones from being hurt when plucking the steel strings. False nails are usually made of celluloid nitrate, tortoise shell or plastic. They should be moderate in thickness, tough and wearable with a smooth surface, such that they can help to pluck the strings for a long period of time.

The false nails can be identical to our own nails in shape, but often look like a pick that is round at the bottom but sharp at the head. We can affix them to our finger pad horizontally (as shown in the right picture) or in a crossed manner with adhesive plaster or bandage, in which the sharp end point outward.

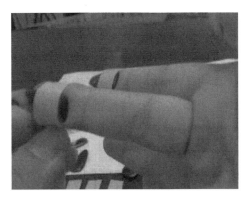

It is more common to wear false nails horizontally with adhesive plaster

Moreover, we should choose those nails designed for adults rather than for kids since the latter are of smaller sizes, and should not fasten them too tightly so as not to hurt our fingers.

Afterwards, we can start playing simple songs, though beforehand we have to learn to read the **numbered musical notation**, which is widely adopted in Chinese sheet music.

The Numbered Music Notation

The sheet music of a Chinese folk song, *Small Birds Worshipping the Phoenix* (小鳥朝鳳), is attached below for demonstrating how to read and interpret sheet music recorded in the numbered music notation:

The numbered music notation, based on the French Galin-Paris-Chevé system, is known as *jianpu* (簡譜) in China and widely adopted in Chinese music publications. Guzheng sheet music is no exception, and thus we must learn to read it or else we cannot play any songs.

<u>General principles</u>

The numbered music notation gets its name because it uses numbers (0 – 7) to represent musical notes, but the numbers indeed tally with the solfeggi directly.   For instance:

1 = do; 2 = re; 3 = mi; 4 = fa; 5 = sol; 6 = la, 7 = si/ti; and 0 = rest irrespective of the key signatures of the sheet music.

Now let's examine the above sheet music in detail:

1) The name of the song (*Small Birds Worshipping the Phoenix*) is written at the top;

2) The origin (*Henan Classical Music*) and arranger (*Arranged by CAO Zheng*) of the song are written at the top-right corner;

3) The key signature (1 = D), time signature (2/4) and tempo ($\flat = 110$) of the song are all written at the top-left corner;

4) The small number inside the bracket indicates the current bar number (the 6th, 12th, 18th, 24th, 30th and 34th bars, all of which are the last bar of every line, are marked accordingly).   The bars are usually arranged in the order of a number's multiple (like there are 6 bars per line in this sheet music), but the actual arrangement depends on the number of notes present within a bar.   More notes will lead to fewer bars per line; and

5) The following signs carry the same meaning in both staff and numbered music notations.

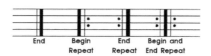

| End | Begin Repeat | End Repeat | Begin and End Repeat |

The key signature

The key signature is indicated by the expression 1 = X for majors and 6 = X for minors. Nonetheless, the minor notation is never used as far as I have observed. As such, this song is recorded in the D major as indicated by the expression 1 = D.

The octaves are represented by adding dots above or below a number. A dot below lowers the note concerned by an octave, whereas a dot above raises it by an octave. For example, 1˙ is at an octave higher than 1 whereas 1̣ is at an octave lower than 1.

The sharp (♯) sign raises a note by a semi-tone and the flat (♭) sign lowers a note by a semi-tone, whereas the natural (♮) sign neutralizes any sharps or flats from preceding notes or the key signature.

The time signature

The time signature is represented by fractions such as 2/4, 4/4, 6/8, which mean that there are 2 quarter notes per bar, 4 quarter notes per bar and 6 eighth notes per bar respectively. In this song, there are 2 quarter notes per bar as indicated by the fraction 2/4.

The tempo

The tempo, if any, will be written next to the time signature in the form of ♪ = X, which means that there are X quarter notes per minute. In this song, ♪ = 110 means that there are 110 quarter notes per minute. Sometimes, you may find a symbol ⫟, which means "Ad libitum". Though stated as free in such cases, the tempo is often defined as per the requirements of individual songs.

The note value

Underlined notes will have their lengths decreased by half per underline they have. For instance, in Bar 2 the length of the first quarter note (solfeggio 1) is reduced by half and becomes an eighth note, and the second eighth note (solfeggio 1) is further reduced by half and becomes a sixteenth note. On the contrary, notes followed by dots will have their lengths increased by half per dot they have (like the first and third eighth notes (solfeggi 2) in Bar 13). If they are followed by a hyphen instead of a dot, their lengths will be doubled.

Though absent in the above sheet music, dynamics (*p, f, mf, mp, ff, pp*), hairpins crescendos, diminuendos and diminuendos will be written below the notes if necessary.

On top of these, there are also guzheng-specific marks instructing us how to play the notes. A list of musical symbols commonly found in guzheng sheet music is attached below (Due to the absence of English equivalents, transliteration, i.e. the *pinyin*, is used for the names of some skills):

Relating to the left hand

Symbol	Name	Meaning
∿∿∿∿∿ ∿∿∿∿	Tremolo (small and large)	While plucking a string with the right hand, slightly shake the string up and down with the left index and middle fingers beyond the goose pillar at a fast pace. Double tildes indicate larger amplitude and hence larger force should be applied
♪ ⌢	Glissando (upward)	Pluck a string with the right hand. Then, press the string with the left hand and hold it for a while until producing the next note. The horizontal sign tells us to cater for the time value at the same time
↳ ⌒	Glissando (downward)	Press a string with the left hand, and then slowly release it while plucking the string with the right hand. The horizontal sign tells us to cater for the time value at the same time
⇜ ⇝	Vibrato	Combine the upward and downward glissandos together by pressing the string with larger amplitude to produce a wave-like note
⑥ ⅰ	*An*	Press the string with the note designated by the circle to produce the main note below. For instance, press the 7th string (solfeggio 6) to produce the solfeggio 1 in this case
▽ ↓	*Dian*	Upon or after plucking a string with the right hand, touch the string gently beyond the goose pillar and remove the finger at once to make the note waver

⊕	Pillar sound	While plucking a string with the right hand, press the head of the goose pillar with the left index finger to produce a dull sound
O	Harmonics	Press the string at 1/2 of the distance between the front Yueshan and the goose pillar to produce a natural harmonic, the pitch of which is at an octave above the original note

Relating to the right hand

The eight basic techniques involving one finger

Symbol	Name	Meaning
L ⊔	*Tuo*	Pluck the string outward with the thumb
⊓ ⊓	*Pi*	Pluck the string inward with the thumb
＼	*Mo*	Pluck the string inward with the index finger
／	*Tiao*	Pluck the string outward with the index finger
⌒	*Gou*	Pluck the string inward with the middle finger
⌣	*Ti*	Pluck the string outward with the middle finger
∧	*Da*	Pluck the string inward with the ring finger
⊤ ∨	*Zhai*	Pluck the string outward with the ring finger

Variations from the basic techniques

Symbol	Name	Meaning
⌐⊔	*Shuang tuo*	Similar to *Tuo*, but pluck two strings quickly instead of only one string
⌐⊓	*Shuang pi*	Similar to *Pi*, but pluck two strings quickly instead of only one string
⧵⧵	*Shuang mo*	Similar to *Mo*, but pluck two strings quickly instead of only one string
∥	*Shuang tiao*	Similar to *Tiao*, but pluck two strings quickly instead of only one string
⌢	*Shuang gou*	Similar to *Gou*, but pluck two strings quickly instead of only one string
⌣	*Shuang ti*	Similar to *Ti*, but pluck two strings quickly instead of only one string
⋀	*Shuang da*	Similar to *Da*, but pluck two strings quickly instead of only one string
⋁	*Shuang zhai*	Similar to *Zhai*, but pluck two strings quickly instead of only one string
⌐⊟	*Zhong tuo*	Similar to *Tuo*, but pluck three strings quickly instead of only one string
⌐---	*Lian tuo*	Similar to *Tuo*, but pluck several strings instead of only one string
⊢ ⊻	*Yao*	Pluck the string outward rapidly with the thumb (the ⊢ sign) and the index finger (the ⊻ sign) respectively
✳	Fluttering finger	Pluck several strings outward rapidly with the thumb

Symbol	Name	Meaning
⊏	*Da cuo*	Perform *Tuo* and *Gou* simultaneously on two strings of which the pitches usually differ by an octave
⊵	*Xiao ti*	Perform *Tuo* and *Mo* simultaneously on two strings
⁄'⟍	*Sanzhi Lun*	Pluck a string inward with the middle and index fingers and then outward with the thumb rapidly
-¦-	*Sizhi Lun*	Pluck a string inward with the ring, middle and index fingers and then outward with the thumb rapidly
↑ ↓	Arpeggio	Pluck the strings with the ring, middle and index fingers and then the thumb rapidly from the high-pitched to low-pitched region or vice versa
⟍ ⟋	*Sao*	Pluck the strings inward or outward rapidly at the low-pitched region with the index, middle, ring and little fingers together as if only one note were produced that sounds like hitting a gong[4]
✗	*Pai*	Hit the strings with the palm to produce sounds like beating a drum
↳	*Bu*	Press a string with the index and middle fingers and pluck it outward with the thumb to produce a sound like hitting a wooden fish

---

[4]   The Gong is a Chinese musical instrument of the percussion family that resembles a flat and circular metal disc, which is hit with a mallet.

⊥	Rest	Press the string with the palm side immediately after plucking it to stop any reverberations
5	Scratch up	Scratch the strings quickly with the index or middle finger from the low-pitched to high-pitched region, or from the lower to higher note as indicated
2	Scratch down	Scratch the strings quickly with the thumb from the high-pitched to low-pitched region, or from the higher to lower note as indicated
/	Scratch up (pillar)	Scratch the strings quickly with the index or middle finger in an upward direction at the left side of the goose pillars
\	Scratch down (pillar)	Scratch the strings quickly with the thumb in a downward direction at the left side of the goose pillars

The list is not exhaustive owing to the plethora of guzheng-specific marks – for example, the eight basic techniques of the right hand already give rise to many combinations that are not shown therein. The descriptions of most right hand skills listed in the above table should speak for themselves, while the majority of the left hand skills are ornamental in nature, which are more difficult and not intended for the beginner level. In the meantime, if you are able to read the above sheet music without any trouble, we can move on to the next stage to learn how to play songs in different key signatures.

The Key Signatures of the Guzheng

The diagram below shows the 21 strings of a guzheng with their vibrating lengths, musical notes and solfeggi under the D major:

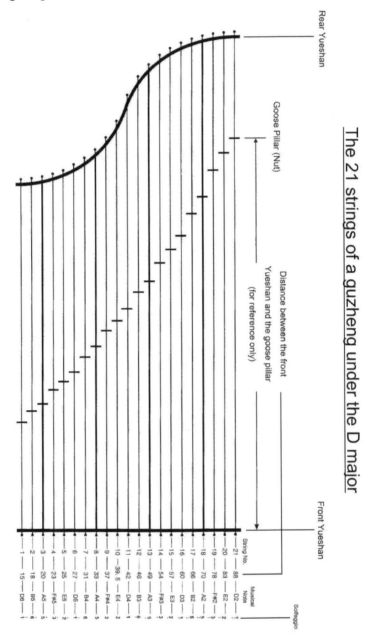

The 21 strings of a guzheng under the D major

The goose pillars can be set at the distances (all measured in cm) as indicated in the above diagram, and then we need to pluck every string to see whether their sound is correct with the aid of a tuner. In case an individual string is slightly out of tune, we can move the goose pillar leftward or rightward to alter the vibrating length and hence the pitch of the note; if the deviation is too large, we have to twist the tuning peg with the tuning key.

Upon adjustment, the key signature under this setting is the D major. For the sake of simplicity, the parameters are tabulated as follows:

The D major (default)

String	1st	2nd	3rd	4th	5th	6th	7th
Note	D6	B5	A5	F#5	E5	D5	B4
Solfeggio	1	6	5	3	2	1	6

String	8th	9th	10th	11th	12th	13th	14th
Note	A4	F#4	E4	D4	B3	A3	F#3
Solfeggio	5	3	2	1	6	5	3

String	15th	16th	17th	18th	19th	20th	21st
Note	E3	D3	B2	A2	F#2	E2	D2
Solfeggio	2	1	6	5	3	2	1

The D major is the default key signature of the guzheng. In order to switch to other majors, we have to move the goose pillars (nuts) on the front panel to alter the lengths of the open strings and hence the notes produced. This is rather different from the erhu and pipa families, of which the nuts are fixed and we change the vibrating lengths by pressing the strings with our left-hand fingers.

To understand how the mechanism works, we are going to look at the seven common key signatures of the guzheng (D, G, C, F, B♭, A and E) and the corresponding notes/ solfeggi.

Solfeggio / Note	1 (do)	2 (re)	3 (mi)	5 (sol)	6 (la)
D major	D	E	F♯	A	B
G major	G	A	B	D	E
C major	C	D	E	G	A
F major	F	G	A	C	D
B♭ major	B♭	C	D	F	G
A major	A	B	C♯	E	F♯
E major	E	F♯	G♯	B	C♯

Let's rearrange the table to show the notes only:

Key	Note (irrespective of the solfeggio)				
D major	D	E	F♯	A	B
G major	D	E	G	A	B
C major	D	E	G	A	C
F major	D	F	G	A	C
B♭ major	D	F	G	B♭	C
A major	C♯	E	F♯	A	B
E major	C♯	E	F♯	G♯	B

And thereby we will change the D major to others progressively.

The G major

From the above table, we can see that by raising the F♯ note of the D major by a semitone to the G note, we will change the key signature to the G major. This can be done by moving the goose pillars of the 4th, 9th, 14th and 19th strings toward the front Yueshan (to the right) by a semitone, by which their vibrating lengths decrease while their pitches increase. The resulting notes and solfeggi are as follows:

String	1st	2nd	3rd	4th	5th	6th	7th
Note	D6	B5	A5	G5	E5	D5	B4
Solfeggio	5	3	2	1	6	5	3

String	8th	9th	10th	11th	12th	13th	14th
Note	A4	G4	E4	D4	B3	A3	G3
Solfeggio	2	1	6	5	3	2	1

String	15th	16th	17th	18th	19th	20th	21st
Note	E3	D3	B2	A2	G2	E2	D2
Solfeggio	6	5	3	2	1	6	5

The C major

Further raising the B note of the G major by a semitone to the C note, we will change the key signature to the C major. This can be done by moving the goose pillars of the 2nd, 7th, 12th and 17th strings toward the front Yueshan (to the right) by a semitone, by which their vibrating lengths decrease while their pitches increase. The resulting notes and solfeggi are as follows:

String	1st	2nd	3rd	4th	5th	6th	7th
Note	D6	C6	A5	G5	E5	D5	C5
Solfeggio	2	1	6	5	3	2	1

String	8th	9th	10th	11th	12th	13th	14th
Note	A4	G4	E4	D4	C4	A3	G3
Solfeggio	6	5	3	2	1	6	5

String	15th	16th	17th	18th	19th	20th	21st
Note	E3	D3	C3	A2	G2	E2	D2
Solfeggio	3	2	1	6	5	3	2

The F major

Further raising the E note of the C major by a semitone to the F note, we will change the key signature to the F major. This can be done by moving the goose pillars of the 5th, 10th, 15th and 20th strings toward the front Yueshan (to the right) by a semitone, by which their vibrating lengths decrease while their pitches increase. The resulting notes and solfeggi are as follows:

String	1st	2nd	3rd	4th	5th	6th	7th
Note	D6	C6	A5	G5	F5	D5	C5
Solfeggio	6	5	3	2	1	6	5

String	8th	9th	10th	11th	12th	13th	14th
Note	A4	G4	F4	D4	C4	A3	G3
Solfeggio	3	2	1	6	5	3	2

String	15th	16th	17th	18th	19th	20th	21st

Note	F3	D3	C3	A2	G2	F2	D2
Solfeggio	1	6	5	3	2	1	6

The B♭ major

Further raising the A note of the F major by a semitone to the B♭ note, we will change the key signature to the B♭ major. This can be done by moving the goose pillars of the 3rd, 8th, 13th and 18th strings toward the front Yueshan (to the right) by a semitone, by which their vibrating lengths decrease while their pitches increase. The resulting notes and solfeggi are as follows:

String	1st	2nd	3rd	4th	5th	6th	7th
Note	D6	C6	B♭5	G5	F5	D5	C5
Solfeggio	3	2	1	6	5	3	2

String	8th	9th	10th	11th	12th	13th	14th
Note	B♭4	G4	F4	D4	C4	B♭3	G3
Solfeggio	1	6	5	3	2	1	6

String	15th	16th	17th	18th	19th	20th	21st
Note	F3	D3	C3	B♭2	G2	F2	D2
Solfeggio	5	3	2	1	6	5	3

The A major

On the contrary, if we lower the D note of the D major by a semitone to the C♯ note, we will change the key signature to the A major. This can be done by moving the goose pillars of the 1st, 6th, 11th, 16th and 21st strings toward the rear Yueshan (to the left) by a semitone, by which their vibrating lengths increase while their pitches decrease. The resulting notes and solfeggi are as follows:

String	1st	2nd	3rd	4th	5th	6th	7th
Note	C#6	B5	A5	F#5	E5	C#5	B4
Solfeggio	3	2	1	6	5	3	2

String	8th	9th	10th	11th	12th	13th	14th
Note	A4	F#4	E4	C#4	B3	A3	F#3
Solfeggio	1	6	5	3	2	1	6

String	15th	16th	17th	18th	19th	20th	21st
Note	E3	C#3	B2	A2	F#2	E2	C#2
Solfeggio	5	3	2	1	6	5	3

The E major

Further lowering the A note of the A major by a semitone to the G♯ note, we will change the key signature to the E major. This can be done by moving the goose pillars of the 3rd, 8th, 13th and 18th strings toward the rear Yueshan (to the left) by a semitone, by which their vibrating lengths increase while their pitches decrease. The resulting notes and solfeggi are as follows:

String	1st	2nd	3rd	4th	5th	6th	7th
Note	C#6	B5	G♯5	F#5	E5	C#5	B4
Solfeggio	6	5	3	2	1	6	5

String	8th	9th	10th	11th	12th	13th	14th
Note	G♯4	F#4	E4	C#4	B3	G♯3	F#3

Solfeggio	3	2	1	6	5	3	2

String	15th	16th	17th	18th	19th	20th	21st
Note	E3	C♯3	B2	G♯2	F#2	E2	C♯2
Solfeggio	1	6	5	3	2	1	6

The semitones

You may notice that the above tables include no semitones (such as the solfeggi "4" and "7"), which were absent in the traditional Chinese pentatonic scale. To produce them, we have to press the strings with our left hand, by which we change their tension and hence the notes produced. For instance, under the D major, we can press the 4th, 9th, 14th and 19th strings to the left of their goose pillars (around 16 to 20 cm toward the rear Yueshan) to produce the solfeggio "4", and the 2nd, 7th, 12th and 17th strings in the same way but with larger force to produce the solfeggio "7". We can locate the semitones with the aid of a tuner and grasp this feeling so that we can later reproduce them on our own. Don't attempt to trace them by sliding the fingers on the strings, but rather learn to pinpoint them immediately.

Pressing the strings with the left hand to produce the solfeggi "4" (left) and "7" (right)

40

Producing notes of the next higher pitch on strings

Similar to the principle of producing semitones, we often produce notes of the next higher pitch (usually within a minor third) on a string instead of utilizing the adjacent string that produces the required note, with a view to expressing the unique flavor of certain songs and facilitating performances. This technique is denoted above as "*An*".

In this regard, the notes that can be produced therewith are summarized as follows:

The solfeggio "2" from all strings that originally produce the solfeggio "1" (apart from each other by a major second);
the solfeggio "3" from all strings that originally produce the solfeggio "2" (apart from each other by a major second);
the solfeggio "5" from all strings that originally produce the solfeggio "3" (apart from each other by a minor third);
the solfeggio "6" from all strings that originally produce the solfeggio "5" (apart from each other by a major second); and
the Solfeggio "1" from all strings that originally produce the solfeggio "6" (apart from each other by a minor third).

In the cases with a separation of a minor third, we need to press even further to the right of the goose pillar on the string with the left hand, and the force required to pluck it with the right hand will be the largest when compared with the cases of a major second and those semitones.

In the end, let's play some songs to practice what we have learnt so far!

Selected Songs

Moon above Mountain Pass (關山月)

Moon above Mountain Pass

Lady Meng Jiang (孟姜女)

Lady Meng Jiang

Bees Flying through Flowers (穿花蜂)

Bees Flying through Flowers

1 = D 2/4

Adagio

Arranged by QIU Dacheng

Buddha's Chant (千聲佛)

Buddha's Chant

1 = D 4/4

Adagio

Composed by LIANG Tsai-ping
Arranged by CAO Zheng

Consort Yu (Yu the Beauty)

Arranged by QU Yun

1 = D 2/4

♩ = 60

On the Golden Hill In Beijing

Tibetan Folk Song
Arranged by QIU Dacheng

1＝D ²⁄₄

Moderato, dolcemente

Online Materials

To know better the melodies of the above selected songs for practicing purposes, please refer to the YouTube videos below:

Moon Over Mountain Pass（關山月）：
https://www.youtube.com/watch?v=zEItA9mNaxo

Lady Meng Jiang（孟姜女）：
https://www.youtube.com/watch?v=InmJ0cJnKc0

Bees Flying through Flowers（穿花蜂）：
https://www.youtube.com/watch?v=pVsfA1SpR0w

Buddha's Chant（千聲佛）：
https://www.youtube.com/watch?v=UlH953pJ-g8

Consort Yu / Yu the Beauty（虞美人）：
https://www.youtube.com/watch?v=jl3rnj6EWB0

On the Golden Hill in Beijing（在北京的金山上）：
https://www.youtube.com/watch?v=yu_kmEJkpcM

Small Birds Worshipping the Phoenix（小鳥朝鳳）：
https://www.youtube.com/watch?v=RpK35n2m7dU

Printed in Great Britain
by Amazon